LAYS OF BOETHIUS

Alfred the Great,
King of England

Translated by: *Walter John Sedgefield*
Edited by: *D.P. Curtin*

Dalcassian
Publishing
Company

PHILADELPHIA, PA

LAYS OF BOETHIUS

Library of Congress Cataloging-in-Publication Data

PRELUDE

Thus the old tale Alfred told us,
West Saxons' king. He showed the cunning,
The craft of songmen. Keenly he longed
Unto the people to put forth songs
To make men merry, manifold stories,
Lest a weariness should ward away
The man self-filled, that small heed takes
Of such in his pride. Again I must speak,
Take up my singing, the tale far known
Weave for mortals; let who will listen.

I

Twas long ago when the eastern Goths
Sent from Scythia their swarms of shieldmen,
With multitudes harried many a nation.
Two tribes triumphant tramped to the south.
The Goths in greatness grew year by year;
Akin to the clansmen kings were there twain,
Raedgod and Aleric; they ruled in power.
Over Jove's mountain came many a Goth
Gorged with glory, greedy to wrestle
In fight with foemen. The banner flashing
Fluttered on the staff. Freely the heroes
All Italy over were eager to roam,
The wielders of bucklers, bearing onward
Even from Jove's mount on to ocean,
Where in sea-streams Sicily lies,
That mighty island, most famous of lands.
Rudely the Roman rule was shattered;
The shieldmen sacked the glorious city
Rome was ravaged; Raedgod and Aleric
Carried the fortress. Away fled the Caesar,
Yes, and his princes, off to the Greeks.
The luckless left ones, losing the combat,
To the Gothic foemen gave up all,
Unwilling forfeited their fathers' treasures,
Their holy allegiance hard was the loss!

The hearts of the heroes held with the Greeks,
If they dared follow the folk's foemen.
Thus things stood the folk was stressed
Many a winter, till Weird appointed
That Theodoric the thanes and nobles
Should lord it over. This leader of them
Was claimed by Christ, the king himself
Brought to baptism a blessed day
For the sons of Rome. They sought right soon
Help from the high one; he then vowed
To give the Romans all rights olden,
Safe to sojourn in their wealthy city,
While God him granted the Goths' dominion
To own and possess. All this the prince broke.
Oath after oath; Arian error
He loved better than the law of the Lord.
The good Pope John he judged in his anger,
Robbed of his head; a heinous deed!
Countless wrongs were likewise wrought
By the Gothic leader on each of the good.
In those days a leader in Rome was living,
A high-born chieftain, cherishing his lord,
While that the high-seat was held by the Greeks;
A man most righteous. He was 'mid the Romans
A giver of treasure glorious ever,
Wise toward this world, wishful of honour,
Learned in booklore; Boethius the name was
That this hero had, that so highly was famed.
Time after time he turned in his mind
The evil and insult by alien princes
Grievously given. To the Greeks he was true,
Remembering the honours and ancient rights
By his fathers aforetime fully enjoyed,
Their love and kindness. Then with cunning
He planned and brooded how he might bring
The Greeks to his country, that once more the Caesar
Might have full power over his people.
Then to their former lords letters of embassy

He sent in secret, summoning them by God,
By their former faith, forthwith to him
To speed Romewards; Greek senators
Should rule the Romans, their rights render
Free to the folk. When he found this out,
Theodoric the Amuling, the thane he had seized,
Charging the braves that did his bidding
To hold fast the hero; fierce was his heart,
The chieftain dreading. Deep in a dungeon
Bolted and barred he bade them cast him.
Then was the man's mood mightily troubled,
The mind of Boethius. Long had he borne
High state worldly; the harder it was
Bravely to bear this bitter fortune.
Sad was the hero he hoped for no mercy,
Locked in prison; past all comfort
On the floor he fell with his face downwards,
Woefully spread, his sorrow speaking,
Hopeless utterly, ever thinking
He should linger in fetters. He called on the Lord
With cheerless voice, and thus he chanted.

II

Ah! many a lay once so merrily
I sang in my joy. Now must I sighing,
Worn with weeping, a woeful outcast,
Sing words of sorrow. Me has this sobbing
And this wailing dazed, so that no more little songs
Can I compose so impressively, though many tales
Once I wove, when I was happy.
Often now I find not the words familiar,
I that in old times often made strange ones.
Me, nearly blind, have these worldly blessings
Drawn in my folly to this dim cavern,
And robbed me entirely of reason and comfort
With their false faith, when I had fain ever
To them trusted. To me they have turned
Their backs, oh! cruelly, and kept joy from me.

Ah! why were you minded, my friends of this world,
In speech or in song to say I was happy
Here in this world? The words are not true ones.
For worldly blessings abide not always.

III

Ah! it is fearful and fathomless deep,
The murky pit where the mind toils,
When the blasts of tempests beat against it
Of worldly afflictions; then in its fighting
Its own true light it leaves behind it,
And in woe forgets the weal eternal.
It dashes onward into this world's darkness,
Weary with sorrows. So has it now
This soul befallen, for now it nought knows
Of good before God, but great grief
From the world unfriendly; it wants comfort.

IV

O You Creator of bright constellations,
Of heaven and earth; You on the high-seat
Eternal reign and the round heaven
All swiftly move, and through Your holy might
The lights of heaven make to hear You,
Even as the sun scatters darkness
Of the dark night time through Your strong power,
And with her pale beams the bright stars
The moon does humble, through Your might's moving;
At whiles too she robs the radiant sun
Of his full light, when it befalls
That they come together by close compulsion.
So too the glorious star of morning,
That we by its other name star of evening
Often hear called, You constrain
To follow the way where the sun goes
Every year he must ever travel,
Fare before him. O Father, You send
Long days in summer with heat sultry;

To the winter also wondrous short days
Have You granted. To the trees You give
South-west breezes, when the black tempest
Sprung from the north-east had utterly stript them
Of every leaf with its loathly wind.
Behold, all creatures in the earth's compass
Obey Your hests; the same do they in heaven
With mind and main, save man only;
He oftenest works in despite of Your will.
Ah! You Eternal and You Almighty
Author and Ruler of all creation,
Pity the offspring of Your poor world,
Even this race of men, through Your mighty power.
Why, O God Eternal, grant You ever
That Fate at the will of wicked mortals
Should turn herself on earth so swiftly?
Often to the guiltless great harm she works.
The wicked are seated in worldly kingdoms
Upon their high-seats, trampling the holy
Under their feet; no man may find out
Why Fate falls so foully awry.
So also are hidden here in this world
In many a borough brightest virtues,
Whereas the sinful in every season
Treat most evilly all those others
That are more righteous, to rule more worthy.
False-faced guile long has gone
Wrapt up in wiles. Now here in the world
Oaths basely broken bring no scathe.
If You, O Chieftain, will not check Fate,
But suffer her in self-will to remain,
Then this do I know, that nations will doubt
Far over earth's fields, all but a few.
O my Sovereign, You that see
All worldly creatures, with eyes of kindness
Look on mortals, for they are moiling,
Battling here in the world's billows,
Poor folk of the earth; pity them therefore.

V

You may by the sun see most clearly,
And by each of the other orbs of heaven
That shine most brightly over the boroughs,
If a dark cloud comes before them
They cannot give forth such a bright gleam
Till the thick mist grow thinner before them.
So too the south breeze fiercely stirs
The calm grey ocean clear as glass;
Then mighty billows mingle the waters,
Stir the whale-sea; fierce waxes ocean
That but shortly before was blithe to look on.
Often too the well-spring is wont to trickle
From the hoar cliff, cool and sparkling,
And onward flowing a straight course follows,
To its home fleets, till there falls upon it
A rock from the mountain, that lies in its midst
Rolled from the peak; parted in twain
The rill is broken, the brook's clear water
Stirred and clouded; the stream is turned
Away from its course, cleft into runnels.
So now the darkness that dims your heart
Wishes to turn back the light of my teaching,
And sorely trouble your spirit's thoughts.
But if you are willing, as well you may be,
The light of the truth clearly to learn,
The brightness of faith, then shall you forsake
Vain surfeit of pleasure, profitless joys.
You shall too forsake the evil fear
Of worldly afflictions, nor wax ever for them
Utterly hopeless; no, nor have yourself
Weakened with wealth, lest with it you be
Brought to sorrow through the sin of pride,
And too puffed up by prosperous fortune,
By joys of the world. Nor again too feebly
Lose all your faith in future good,
When in this world the weight of afflictions

Bears on you sorely, and you are beset
With utter terror; for ever it tides
That a man's breast is bound most firmly
With dire confusion if either of these dangers
Here may trouble him, torture his spirit.
For both these hardships hand in hand,
A mist misleading draw over the mind,
So that the sun eternal its light may not send forth
For the black mists until these be blown away.

VI

Then Wisdom again unlocked her word-hoard.
Her tale of sooth sang in these words:
'While the bright sun most clear is beaming,
Gleaming in heaven, gloom enwraps
Over the world all other bodies;
For their light is nought, nothing at all,
When set against the sun's great brightness.
When softly blows from south and west
The wind beneath heaven, then soon wax
The flowers of the field, fain to be able.
But the stiff storm-wind, when it strongly blows
From out of the north-east, how soon it nips
The rose's beauty! By the northern blast
The spacious ocean is helpless spurned
Till strongly heaving it strikes the beach.
Alas, that in the world nothing wears
Firm and lasting long on this earth.

VII

Then did Wisdom follow her wont,
Glee-words chanted, changed song for speech,
Of tales of sooth sang yet another:
'Never on high hill had she ever heard
That any of men might make to stand
A roof-fast hall; nor need any hope
To have the wit to mingle wisdom,
To put it together with pride overweening.

Heard you ever that any of mortals
On hills of sand his house could establish
Firm to last him? Nor can any mortal
Build up wisdom, where the hill-side
Is spread with covetise. Quickly the rain
Is sucked by the sand; so do the great ones,
With their bottomless greed of goods and glory.
They drink to the dregs this dross so fleeting,
Yet the thirst of their craving is never cooled.
A man may not build a house on a mountain
That may long tarry; soon the tempest
Swift on it sweeps. Sand is useless
In deluge of rain to him that dwells
In the house as master; it melts away,
In the rain sinks. So with every man;
His inmost mind is mightily shaken,
Stirred from its station, when the strong winds,
Of earthly troubles toss and tease it,
Or when the ruthless rain of affliction,
Boundless distress, dashes upon it.
But he that ever wishes to own
True joy eternal must turn and flee
This world's beauty. Then let him build
The house of his soul so that he find
The Rock of Humility, hard and fastest,
Sure foundation; he shall not slip
Though that the tempest of worldly troubles
Or flood of worries fiercely assail it.
For in that Vale of the Lowly the Lord Himself
Ever abides, owns His Home;
And there too Wisdom in memory waits.
A life without sorrow he always leads
That chooses wisdom; it never changes,
Since he disdains delights of the world,
From every evil utterly free;
He hopes in eternity hereafter to come.
Him then everywhere God Almighty
Keeps always, ever unceasing,

Fast abiding in the blessed joys
Of his own mind, through the Master's grace,
Though often the winds of worldly troubles
Batter and bruise him, or never bating
Cares be fretting, when the fierce gusts
Of worldly blessings blow unkindly,
Though him ever the endless worry
Of earthly fortune sore confound him.'

VIII

After Wisdom these words had spoken,
Clearly set forth, soon she began
Sooth words to sing, and thus she spoke
'Oh! the ancient days for all earth-dwellers
Throughout the world were ever the best.
Then was each man ever contented
With fruits of the earth; 'tis otherwise now.
Not then in the world were wealthy homes,
Nor many kinds of meat and drink;
Nor anything of raiment recked men then,
In these days to men of all things dearest;
For then such was not seen as yet,
Never the sea-folk had seen it at all.
No, nor anywhere of it had heard.
Ah! then the sin of lust they longed not to do,
But in degree they duly followed
The call of nature as Christ appointed.
But one meal daily they always made
Of the earth's increase, at hour of even,
Of plants of the wood. No wine they drank
Bright from the bowl; none could boast
Skill to mingle drink with his meat,
Water with honey, nor to fashion by sewing
Clothing of silk; nor had they cunning
In costly stuffs; nor stood there halls
Cleverly planned; but it was their custom
In every season to sleep in the open
In the deep tree-shade. They drank burn-water

Cool from the spring. Never did chapman
See over the sea-surge the shore of strange land;
Nor had men heard of the harrying ship-host
No, nor was fighting familiar to mortals.
Not as yet was the earth anywhere stained
With the blood of a man nor the dye of the blade,
Nor even one wounded had any man witnessed
Under the sun. So too none was worthy
Held in the world if his will seemed
Evil unto men; by all was he loathed.
Oh! were it true, or would God but grant
That here on earth in our days now,
Over the wide world, man's wont was such
Under the sun! But now 'tis more sinful,
For covetous greed so clogs the soul
Of every man that he heeds not other things.
And in the mind boiling it burns ever,
This curse of covetise, never contented,
Black and bottomless blazes smouldering,
Even as the mountain that mortals call
By name of Etna; this on an island,
Even Sicily, with sulphur burns,
Hell-fire widely hight by mortals,
For unceasing it smoulders ever,
And all around it the rest of the land
It fiercely blasts with blaze consuming.
Ah! who was the first that filled with greed
Dwelt in the world, and dug the ground
In quest of gold and curious jewels?
Wealth did he find, fatal to many,
In the world hidden in water or earth.

IX
We all have heard what hateful deeds
Far and near Nero wrought,
King of the Romans, when that his rule
Was first under heaven, fatal to many.
The fierce one's madness men widely knew,

His lawless lust and laches unnumbered,
His sins and murders, misdeeds many,
The cursed wiles of that wicked one.
He bade for his sport with fire destroy
The city of Rome that was the seat
Of full dominion, for in his folly
He fain would try whether the fire,
Flaming brightly, would burn as long,
Would rage as red, as the Romans told
That Troy town was of old overtaken
By the brightest of flames that longest burned
In homes under heaven. A hideous thing,
To take his pleasure in such perilous sport.
Nought else gaining, this only regarding,
To make his power far over peoples
Widely renowned, over the nations.
It likewise betided once on a time
That this same man sent to murder
All the rulers of the Senate of Rome,
And all the best by birth as well
That he could find among his folk;
And his own brother besides he bade,
Yes, and his mother, be murdered with swords,
Killed with blade-edge. He himself butchered
His bride with the brand, and ever was blither,
Gayer of mood, the more of such murder,
Such hateful wrong, he wrought on mortals.
Nought did he heed whether hereafter
The mighty Master would mete out vengeance,
Wreak on the wicked their wrongful deeds,
But in his soul was glad of his guile and sins,
Bloodthirsty ever. But notwithstanding,
He governed all of this glorious world,
Where air and sea encircle the land
And the deep sea enrings this realm of mortals,
The seats of men, south, east and west,
Right to the northmost nesses of earth.
All bowed to Nero, for need or pleasure

None was there of men but must obey him.
When his pride was highest 'twas a pretty jest
How the kings of the earth he killed and harried!
Do you gainsay that God Almighty
Could most readily wrest his power
From the boastful scourge, and strip him bare
Of all dominion through the might eternal,
Or utterly curb the course of his sins?
Oh, that He would only, as He easily might,
All such felony fain forbid him!
Oh, 'twas no light yoke which that lord planted,
A grievous annoy, on the necks of his thanes,
Of all his lieges that in his lifetime
Over this brittle world were fated to bide
He with the gore of guiltless men
Fouled his sword-blade, full many's the time.
Thus we see clearly, as we have often said,
That dominion can do no good
If he that has gained it have no good will.

X

If any living man longs for glory,
And fame without gain would fain have for his own,
Then with my words would I beseech him
On all sides about him far out to spy,
Clearly to look, south, east, and west,
And consider how broad with the clouds all about
Is the vault of the sky. So may the wise man
Easily deem this earth of ours
By the side of that other wondrously small,
Though to the witless wide it seems,
To straying men strong in its place.
Yet may the sage deep in his spirit
Feel great shame for the lust of glory,
When the thirst for fame fiercely presses,
Although he may not make it to spread,
In no wise whatever, over these narrow
Quarters of earth. How idle is glory!

Why ever, O proud ones, take you pleasure
To bow your own necks beneath the yoke
Heavy and grievous, glad that you may?
Why do you labour so long in vain,
Aim to possess fame in the world,
Over the nations, more than you need?
Though it befell that southward and north
The uttermost denizens, dwellers of earth,
In many a tongue intoned your praises;
Though you were known for noblest birth,
Worshipped for wealth, waxing in splendour,
Dear for your valour; Death heeds these not
When heaven's Governor gives him leave.
But the wealthy man, and the wanting in goods,
Death makes equal, in all things alike.
Where now are the wise one's, Weland's bones,
The worker in gold, once greatest in glory?
I ask where the bones of Weland are buried
For never any that on earth lives
May lose any virtue lent him by Christ;
Nor may one poor wretch be robbed with more ease
Of his soul's virtue, than may the sun
Be swung from his path, or the swift heavens
Moved from their courses by the might of a man.
Who now is aware of wise Weland's bones,
In what barrow lying they litter the ground?
Where is the senator so mighty of Rome,
The bold champion of whom we chant,
Head of their army, he that the name
Amid the burghers, of Brutus bore?
Where is the wise one that wished for fame,
The people's shepherd, steadfast of purpose,
That was a sage in each thing several,
Keen and the cunning, Cato was called?
Many long days ago these men departed;
No man knows now where they be.
What is left of them but their fame alone?
Too slight is the glory of such teachers.

For they were worthy, were those heroes,
Of more in the world. But worse it is now,
When over the earth, in every quarter,
They and those like them are little spoken of,
And some not a few are clean forgotten,
And their fame cannot keep them longer
Known to all men, noble heroes.
Though you now deem, desire strongly,
That long in the land your life may last,
How ever the better can you be or seem?
For Death no man leaves, though long it seem,
His life-days told, if the Lord it allows.
But what profit does a mortal possess
In this world's glory, if he be gripped
By death everlasting after this life?

XI

There is one Creator, we cannot doubt,
And He controls every creature
Of heaven and of earth, and of the high seas,
And all the things that therein dwell,
Of those unseen, and likewise of such
As with our eyes we are able to see,
Of all creation; Almighty is He.
Him humbly court all things created
That of their service have any knowledge,
And none the less of those that know not
That they minister unto the Master.
In us He created ways and customs,
And for all His creatures peace unaltered,
Never ceasing in its nature,
When that He wished whatever pleased Him,
As long as He liked should live and last.
So it shall be, and for ever abide;
For never they may, the moving creatures,
Cease from their motion, sink into rest,
Swerve from the way that the Warden of heaven
Has appointed for all in order unchanging.

The King of all things has His creation
Bound with His bridle; both has He done,
Governed each one and guided them too,
So that they may not against the Master's will
Ever cease moving, nor ever again
Go any more than the Guarder of glory
Will grant unto them His reins of guidance.
He has with His bridle bound earth and heaven,
And the whole circle of deep sea-waters.
Thus has He curbed, the King of heaven,
With His control, all of His creatures,
So that the one strives with other,
And loath to his fellow fast does cleave,
Firm upholds, fast enclasps,
Lest they dash asunder. For ever their duty
Again to circle on the self-same journey
That at the first the Father appointed,
And ever renewed again to revive.
So is it fashioned, the framework ancient,
That warring in hate the hostile creatures
Fast and for ever firm peace maintain.
Thus fire and water, firm land and ocean,
And things many more, in just the same manner
Over the wide world are warring together;
Yet can they keep their course of service,
Fellowship holding firm and abiding.
Nor is it merely matter of wonder
That things full of hate fare together,
Remaining fellows; more fit for marvel
That none of them ever can live without other,
But every thing made his opposite meets
Under the heavens, that humbles his pride
Before that it grow too great to be borne.
He has, the Almighty, to every creature
Appointed its course that it must keep
Growth for plants, green for leaves
That in autumn later languish and fall.
Winter brings very cold weather;

Swift are its winds; summer then comes,
The warm weather; Lo! the wan night
Is lit by the moon, till the morn is brought
To men by the sun over this spacious world.
He has, the same God, to sea and land
Their boundaries fixed; the flood dares not
Over earth's borders her sway to broaden
For the tribe of fishes, without the Lord's favour;
Nor may she ever the threshold of earth
Lightly overtread; nor may the tides either
Bear the water over earth's borders.
These are the commands that the glorious King,
The Bright Life-Giver, does let while He will
Keep within bounds His noble creatures;
But when the Eternal and the Almighty
Looses the reins that rule all creatures,
Even the bridle wherewith He bound
All that He fashioned at the first creation
(By the bridle we speak of we seek to betoken
The case where things are all conflicting):
If the Lord lets the bridle loosen,
Forthwith they all leave love and peace,
The friendly union of their fellowship.
All things whatever their own will follow,
All world-creatures shall war together,
Till this our earth utterly perish,
And so also other things, in the same fashion,
By their own nature become as nought.
But the same God that governs all things,
Brings together, many folk binds,
And firmly unites in friendship's bonds;
He links in wedlock the love that is pure
In peaceful mateship. So too the Mighty One
Fellow to fellow firmly joins,
So that their friendship forth and for ever
They hold, and their faith fast undoubting,
Their peace unvarying. O God of victory,
Most happy indeed were mankind's lot,

If but their hearts could hold their course
Steadily steered by Your strong might,
And evenly ordered as the others are also,
The world's creatures! Yes, it were truly
Right merry for men, might it so be!

XII

Whoso fertile land fain would till,
Let him promptly pluck from the field
Fern and thorn, and farze-bush also,
The weeds, in all places eager to injure
The wheat clean-sprinkled, lest it sproutless
Should lie on the land. To all folk likewise
This next example no less suits:
The comb of the honey cannot but seem
To each son of men sweeter by half,
If he have tasted before the honey
Anything that is bitter. Even thus also
To every mortal more welcome by far
Is gentle weather, when just before
Storms have assailed him, and the stiff wind
Out of the north-east. No man would reckon
Daylight a blessing if the dark night
Had not for mortals mustered terrors.
So of earth-dwellers to each it seems
That blessedness true is ever the better,
More pleasant by far, the more he of woe,
Of cruel hardships, here endures.
So you the sooner may in your soul
The truest of blessings trace more clearly,
And to their source soonest arrive,
If first and foremost forth from your breast,
Root and branch, you upwrench
Happiness false, even as the farmer
From his field plucks ill weeds a plenty.
Then, I warrant you, you will clearly
Forthwith recognize real blessings,
And you will never have heed for anything else,

When all plainly you do perceive them.

XIII

In song will I again send forth the tidings,
How the Almighty, all things' Ruler,
With bridle urges, bends at will
His creatures with might and due measure,
Marvellous well makes them hold.
The Wielder of heaven has welded together,
Wrapt all his creatures round and about,
Fixed with fetters, so that they fail ever
To find any road to wrest themselves free.
And yet every creature courses along,
Onward bending, bound for its goal,
Seeking the kind that the King of angels,
The Father at first, firmly appointed.
So now all things are thitherward moving,
The spacious creation, save certain angels,
Save man also. Many, too many
Dwellers in the world war with their nature!
Though you a she-lion should meet in the land,
A pleasant creature wondrously tame,
Loving her master with lively affection,
And yet every day dreading him also,
If it befall that savour of blood
She ever tastes, truly none needs
Ever to hope that she will hold fast
To her tameness after; well do I think,
New as it is, no more she will heed it,
But her wild wont will soon remember,
The way of her fathers. Fierce she begins
To rend her fetters, to roar and growl,
And first she bites, before all others,
Her own house-master, and hastily thereafter
Each single man that she may meet
Naught she leaves that owns life,
Nor beast nor man, mangling all she finds.
Thus too the wood-birds, wondrous gentle,

Truly tame, if they come to the trees
In the heart of the holt, soon they heed not
Those that taught them, who long time before
Trained them and tamed them. Wild in the trees
Ever thereafter their ancient nature
They gladly follow, though fain would their teachers
With cunning tricks offer them tempting
Even the food that in former days
To tameness enticed; the twigs so pleasant
Seem to their minds, the meat they heed not,
So pleasant for them when woodland sounds,
When they can hear the piping choir
Of other song-birds; then do they send
Their own notes forth. All together
The sweet song raise; the wood is ringing.
So too with each tree whose nature 'tis
That in the grove it grows highest,
Though that you bend a bough to the ground,
It upward leaps when you leave
The wood to its will; it goes to its kind.
So too the sun when that it sinks,
Noon long past; the shining lamp
Hastens sinking, on his unseen journey
Ventures by night; then in the north-east
To men appears, to earth-dwellers brings
Clear-bright morning, and over men mounts,
Upward ever, until he comes
To the topmost station where he highest stands.
Thus every creature with all its might,
Through this wide world, goes and hastens
With all endeavour, eager to come
Once more to its kind as soon as it can.
On earth there now lives no single creature
That craves not one day to come
Back to its home whence it once came.
Here no care racks, here rest is eternal
'Tis God Almighty, as all men know.
Over the earth now there lives no creature

That spins not round and on itself turns,
Even as a wheel; for it so whirls
That at last it stands in its ancient station
And ever as soon as it has spun round,
When all its round is run to the end,
Then duly again it shall do what it did,
And be yet again what it was of yore.

XIV

What avails the greedy one in earth's goods wealthy,
What boot for his mind, though much he owns
Of gold and of gems, and every thing good,
And countless possessions; and though his ploughs till
Each day for him a thousand acres?
What though this middle-earth, and this race of men,
Under the sun, south, west, and east,
In his dominion are all dependent,
When none of his trappings can he take away from here
Out of this world, no, not one more
Of his hoarded treasures than he brought hither?

XV

Though the unrighteous evil monarch,
Nero the king, decked him anew
In fairest raiment in wondrous fashion,
With gold adorned, and goodly jewels,
Yet through the world by all men of wisdom
In the days of his life he was loathed and scorned,
Filled with all sin. This foe of men
To all his darlings dealt high favours
Yet I cannot conceive how they could hold
Themselves anything the better. Though for a season
He chose them without virtue, this most witless king,
Yet no wise man worshipped them the more.
Though the man of folly make himself king,
How can he reckon, the man of right reason,
That he is anything better, or even so seems?

XVI

He that seeks power must first strive
That he may of himself in his mind within
Lordship compass, lest he may be ever
To his sinful ways utterly subject.
From out of his spirit let him speedily pluck
The manifold cares that carry no profit;
Let him cease a while his mournful sighing
For his evil fortune; though all be his,
This world of ours, wherever begirdled
By ocean-waters, to him only given,
As far away as in the west
Outermost lies an isle in ocean,
Where never is night known in summer,
Nor is the day in winter divided,
Into times parted, Tile (Thule) men call it--
Though that a man be sole master
Of all this island, and from thence onward
Even to the Indies out in the east
Yes, though all this be his own to govern,
How is his might any the more,
If of himself control he has not,
Nor of his thoughts, nor thoroughly strive
Well to beware in word and in deed
Of all the sins of which we were speaking?

XVII

All earth-dwellers one origin had,
All men of the land, one like beginning;
From one pair only all proceeded,
From a man and woman, within the world
And to this day even all men alike,
The base and the high ones, are born in the world.
Nor is that a marvel, for all men know
That there is one God of all world-creatures,
Lord of mankind, Father and Maker.
He the sun lends, light out of heaven,
To moon and stars; on earth He made men,

And brought to the body in the beginning
The soul in union; under the sky
Folk He created all fully equal.
Why are you therefore yourselves over others
Placing ever, proud without reason,
When none you are able to meet not noble?
Why are you boasting now of your birth?
In the mind only of every man lies
The real nobility whereof I reason,
Not in the flesh of the folk of earth.
But every mortal that is utterly,
Merely subject to his sinful ways,
Soonest leaves life's Creator;
Nor does he heed his own high nature,
No, nor the Father that first him fashioned.
For this the Almighty removes his honour,
So that henceforth here in the world
He goes dishonoured, nor comes to glory.

XVIII

Alas! that wrongful unrighteous desire,
Frenzied lewdness leads to this,
That of all mankind it amazes the mind,
Of each and all men, nearly utterly.
Lo! the wild bee is wise of nature,
Yet must perish all in a moment,
If in her anger anything she stings.
So too a man's soul soon shall die,
If that the body becomes baser
By carnal desire, unless there come first
Regret to his heart before he from here goes.

XIX

Oh! sore is the folly, consider it who will,
And full of peril for every person,
That wretched mortals utterly amazes,
And far from the right road rapidly leads
Have you the will to seek in the woodland

Bright red gold among green trees?
Well do I know that no wise man
Will seek it there, since there it is not,
Nor look in vineyards for lustrous gems.
Why do you not hang nets on the hill-tops
When you would fain fishes capture,
Salmon and herrings? It seems likely
That dwellers on earth, all of them, know,
Men of sense, that such live not there.
Will you go hunting, with hounds follow,
In the salt sea, when you would seek
Harts and hinds? Have you not knowledge
That such as these you must seek in forests
More often by far than out in ocean?
Marvellous it is that all men know
That by the sea-shore search must be made,
And by river-beaches, for brightest jewels,
White and crimson, and of every colour.
Yes, they know also where it is needful
Fishes to seek, and many such things,
The wealth of the world. Well they do so,
Men all yearning, year's end to year's end.
But of all things this is most wretched,
That fools have become so utterly blind,
In midst of error, that in mind they cannot
Readily tell where blessings eternal,
Happiness true, are hidden away,
For they will not follow in their footsteps
Nor seek the blessings; robbed of sense,
In this frail life they think to find it,
True Happiness, God Himself.
I know no means whereby I may
Within my breast blame as severely
Such men's folly, as fain I would do
Nor can I tell you with full clearness;
For they are feebler and more foolish,
More severed from blessing, than I can set forth.
Wealth and possessions, these they wish for,

And men's worship they are eager to win.
When they have compassed what their mind craves,
Then do they witless think in their folly
That True Happiness they have at last.

XX
O my Master, You are Almighty,
Great and noble, in glory famous;
And You are wonderful to all with wisdom!
O You God Eternal of all creation,
You have wondrously well created
Unseen creatures, and also those
That are seen of men! Softly You rule
The bright creation with Your craft
And power of wisdom. You to this world
From first beginning forth to the ending
Have dealt out seasons, as it most suited,
In regular order, such that they ever
Are faring out, or else returning.
You Your creatures that cannot move
Unto Your will wisely compel,
Yourself abiding still and stirless,
And unchanging for ever and ever.
None is mightier, none more famous,
Nor midst all creatures is Your match to be found.
And as yet never have You felt need
Of all the works which You have wrought,
But by Your will all You have worked,
And with the power that You possess.
You have made the world and every creature
Yet no need had You, none whatever,
Of all this grandeur. 'Tis great, the nature
Of Your goodness, regard it who will;
For they are one only in every wise,
You and Your goodness. This is Your own,
For not from without to You has it come.
But this I guess surely, that Your goodness is
Goodness almighty, Yourself, O God;

It is unlike ours in nature;
From outside comes all we contain
Of good in the world, from God Himself.
You have no anger to anything conceived,
For to You nothing knows likeness
No, nor even is anything more crafty;
For You all goodness by Your contriving,
Alone in Your counsel carried it out.
Before You there was not any creature
Either to do or to leave undone;
But without pattern, Prince of mankind,
God Almighty, all You wrought,
All very good. You are Yourself
The Highest Good. Ah! You, holy Father,
After Your will the world created,
This earth with Your might made to be,
O Chief of hosts, as You did choose,
And with Your will wield all things.
So You, true God, Yourself grant
All good that is; for long ago
You all Your creatures first created
Strongly alike; yet some there were
Not like in nature. One name You gave,
One name only, to all together,
World under sky. O God of splendour
This single name You parted since,
Father, into four: first the earth,
Second water, part of the world,
Thirdly fire, and fourthly air;
These four together form the world,
Yet each of these four has its own birthplace,
Each possesses its proper station,
Though each of them be with the other
Much commingled, and with the might also
Of the Father Almighty firmly united,
In harmony single, smoothly together,
By Your command, O kindly Father,
So that none of them over another's bounds

Dares trespass, for dread of the Lord,
But these servants together suffer union,
The King's champions, chill with heat,
Wet with dryness; yet are they warring.
Water and earth all increase bring,
Cold in their ways the one and the other
Water wet and cold round the land winds,
The all-green earth, yet either is cold.
Air is a mixture in the midst dwelling;
Nought should we wonder that it is warm and cold,
The wet cloudbank by the wind blended;
For midmost it lies, as men hear tell,
Between fire and earth. Full many know
That highest over earth of all things created
Fire lives, and land is lowest.
Oh, 'tis wonderful, Chief of war-hosts,
That with Your bare thought You bring to pass
That to every creature with clear distinction
You have fixed its marches, yet have not mixed them!
Lo! for the water wet and cold
The land as a floor firm have You laid;
For never quiet, to every quarter
Far would it flow, feeble and yielding;
It would never be able, for a truth do I know,
To stand by itself, but the earth it supports,
And some of it also sucks adown,
So that thereafter it may for the soaking
Be washed with showers. Wherefore leaf and grass
Broad over Britain are blooming and growing,
A boon to mortals. The cold earth brings
Countless fruits of marvellous kinds
For with the water wet it becomes.
But if this were not so, then would it certainly
Dry up to dust, and then be driven
By the wind afar, as often it befalls
That over the land ashes are blown.
On earth nothing were able to live,
Nor would it any more enjoy the water,

Nor dwell in it ever by any device,
For mere coldness, if You, King of angels,
Somewhat with fire the land and sea-stream
Had not mingled, and properly measured
Cold with heat by Your cunning power,
So that fire cannot lurid consume
Earth and sea, though it be seated
Firmly in either, the Father's old work.
None the less marvel to me it seems
That earth and ocean are all unable,
Though both cold creatures, by any contrivance
Fully to quench the fire within them,
Therein planted by the Lord's power.
Now this is a property possessed by waters,
To live upon earth and in the clouds also,
And even on high above the heavens.
Then the rightful region of fire,
Its native home, is high over all creatures
That we may behold over this wide world;
Though it is mingled with every member
Of world-creatures, it cannot avail
To deal to one of them deadly damage,
Save by the leave of our Life-Giver,
Even the Eternal Almighty God.
More heavy is earth than other creatures,
More stoutly welded; for during a space
Beneath creation it nethermost lay,
Save only the firmament that this broad fabric
Outside and around each day circles,
Yet never touches the earth anear,
Nor may it in one place more than another
Nearer reach; round it speeds
Above and beneath, yet equally near.
Every creature whereof we recount
Has for itself its separate home;
Yet is it likewise linked with others,
Nor may one live lonely ever,
Though dimly seen be their dwelling together.

Thus earth in fire and water is found;
The poor of wit have pains to see it,
But to the wise well it is known.
So too is fire fixed fast in water,
And in the stones still it lurks
'Tis hard to see, 'tis there, however.
The Father of angels has bound the fire
So fast and firmly that it cannot fly
Again to the region where the rest of the fire
High over this world in its home dwells.
Soon it forsakes this frail creation,
Overcome by cold, if it seeks its country
Yet every creature craves to go
Where its kin it finds most crowded together.
You have established through Your strong might,
King of war-hosts, in wondrous wise
The earth so firmly that she inclines
Nought to one side, nor may she sink
This way nor that way more than she was wont,
By nought upheld of earthly nature.
It is equally easy upward or downward
For this earth of men to move at will;
This is most like to an egg, where lies
The yolk in the middle, yet the shell moves
Around outside; so stands the world
Still in its station with the streams round it,
The stirring floods, the air and stars,
While the gleaming shell round all glides
Every day, and long has done so.
O God of the nations! of threefold nature
A soul You have given us, that You since
Move and guide through Your strong might,
So that no less thereof lives
In a single finger, even the smallest,
Than in the whole body. But a little ago
I clearly sang that the soul was
In every thane a threefold creature,
For all sages this do say,

That three natures are seen in every soul;
Passion first comes, second desire;
The third is by nature nobler than the others,
Reason we call it; it causes no shame,
For the beasts have it not, but to man it belongs.
Countless creatures contain the two others;
Nearly every beast boasts desire,
And likewise passion each possesses
Wherefore mankind, over the world,
Has other creatures all surpassed;
For what men have the others have not,
Even that single virtue of which we have sung.
This mighty reason in every man
Shall ever subdue desire to itself,
And likewise passion hold in its power.
She with thought the mind of a thane,
And with reflection shall rule in all things.
She has most might in man's spirit,
And is most perfect of all his powers.
Lo! You the Soul, Sender of triumph,
High King of nations, thus did create,
So that it turns and turns about,
Round itself moving, even as all moves,
The swift firmament fleetly whirling,
Every day, by the Lord's great doing,
This earth encircling. So does man's soul
Like to a wheel she whirls round herself,
Ofttimes thinking of that which is earthly,
The Lord's creatures daily and nightly;
Sometimes in thought she seeks herself,
At others gives heed to God Eternal,
Her own Creator. In course she goes
Most like to a wheel, on herself whirling.
When deeply she muses on Him who made her,
Then up she is raised over herself;
But in her own self she ever abides,
When in her fancy she follows herself.
Lastly she falls beneath herself far

When she admires these frail things earthly,
And loves them all more than law eternal.
O God of ages, You gave a home
in heaven to souls; You send them freely
Glorious gifts, God Almighty,
In measure fitting the merits of each
These all are beaming bright in the heavens
In the clear night, but nevertheless
Not equal in light lo! we see often,
When serene is the night, the stars in heaven,
Not all beaming with equal brightness.
O God Everlasting! You did also unite
A thing of heaven to the earthly here,
Soul to body; ever since they abide,
Both the eternal and earthly together,
The soul in the flesh. See, ever to You
They yearn to go from here, for from You hither
They had their source, and shall seek You again.
But the body of man must ever abide
Here on the earth, for coming from her
He grew in the world. Together they were
No longer nor less than to them was allowed
By the Almighty, who ages aforetime
Made them comrades; the true King is He.
He fashioned the land, and filled it thereafter
With manifold races, as men have told me,
And sorts of beasts, mankind's Saviour.
Then did He sow many a seed
Of trees and plants in the tracts of earth.
Grant to our minds, God Eternal,
That they may to You, Master of all things,
Through these miseries mount to heaven,
And from these cares, kindly Father,
Ruler of nations, may rise to You;
That then with eyes open we may be able
With the eyes of the mind, through Your aid mighty,
The fount to gaze on of all goodness,
Yourself to view, victorious God.

Grant strong sight to the gaze of our minds,
That we may on Yourself be able thereafter
To fix them firmly, Father of angels.
Scatter the mist that now for a season
Before the eyes of our understanding
Thickly has hung, heavy and darksome.
Send, we pray You, to our spirits' eyes
Your own light, Ruler of life;
For You are the brightness, benign Father,
Of the true Light; likewise You are Yourself
The firm rest, Father Almighty,
Of all the true ones. Tenderly You suffer
That they may behold You, Yes, Yourself even.
You are of all things, O nations' Ruler,
Beginning and end. O angels' Father,
Of all things You bear the burden lightly,
Never wearied. Yourself are the Way,
Yes, and the Guide, of all things living,
And the goodly Bourne to which the Way bends.
To You all mortals are moving ever,
All men from below, in the bright creation.

XXI

O sons of mankind, over earth moving,
Let each that has freedom find out the way
To the eternal goodness whereof our speech is,
And to the blessings that are our song's burden.
The man that is straitly bound by the sway
Of the worthless love of this world glorious,
Let him right soon seek for himself
Fullness of freedom, that forthwith he may come,
Into the blessings of the Bidder of spirits
For this is the rest from all our wrestling,
The hopeful haven for the high vessels
Of the minds of us men, mild harbour bright.
This is the only haven we ever shall have
After the tossing of troublous billows,
After each tempest, truly peaceful.

This is the sanctuary, the sole comfort
Of all weary mortals, when they are over,
Our worldly troubles; 'tis the pleasant prize
That shall be ours to own after these hardships.
But well do I think, no treasure golden,
No jewel of silver, no gem of cunning,
No wealth of this world will ever illumine
The eyes of the mind; nor do they amend
Their keenness of sight so that they spy
Bliss unfeigned; but they far more
The eyes of the mind of every man
Blind in his breast than make them brighter.
So each of the things that now on earth
In this their life is loved by mankind,
Frail and earthly, fleets away.
But they be wondrous, the Beauty and Brightness
That give brightness and beauty to each,
And possess ever after power over all.
It is not the will nor the wish of the Ruler
That our souls should perish, but He prefers
With light to fill them, life's Controller.
If any creature therefore with his eyes undimmed,
The glance of his spirit, may ever gaze on
The clear brightness of the heavenly beam,
Then will he say that the sun's shining
Is merely darkness to the mind of each man,
If it be measured with the mighty light
Of God Almighty; for every spirit
'Tis ceaseless, eternal, for the souls of the blest.

XXII

He that desires the Right in due measure,
In its inner nature anxious to track,
And know it fully so that none be able
To drive it out, nor anything earthly
Have power to hinder: first him behoves
In his own soul to seek what he earlier
During a season sought from without.

Then let him bring it forth from his bosom,
And leave behind, as long as he may,
Every sorrow that serves for nought;
And let him muster with might and with main
Each thought within him to that end only.
Let him say to his mind, that it may find
Within itself only all that it now
Oftenest seeks ever outside,
Every goodness. Then he gets to know
Things evil and idle, all that he had,
Hid in his bosom so long before,
Even as clearly as he can the sun
Behold with the eyes of this present body
And he moreover his mind perceives
Lighter and brighter than is the beaming
Of the sun in summer, when the sky's jewel,
Sheer orb of heaven, shines brightest.
So neither the sins nor laziness of the body,
Nor its foul vices, are fully able
To wrest from the mind its righteous nature
In any mortal. Though that a man
By the sins of his body, and by its laziness also,
And by vice be assailed for many a season,
And though that his mind be grievously marred
With the foul curse of careless folly,
And a fog of error float before
The dreary spirit of the sons of men,
So that it cannot shine at all so clearly
As it would do if it were able,
Yet there remains ever retained
Some seed of the truth in the soul of man,
So long as united it lives with body.
This corn of seed is ever quickened
By means of inquiry, and afterwards also
With good teaching, if it is to grow.
How may any man make out an answer
To anything asked, by aid of reason,
Though others ask him after it righteously,

Closely inquiring, if he contains
In his own mind neither much nor little
Of righteousness in him nor anything of reason?
Yet no man lives that is so lacking,
So utterly robbed and void of reason,
That he is unable the answer to find
Locked in his breast if others beg him.
For this is true, the proverb that our Plato,
The ancient sage, once said unto us:
'Each man,' he said, 'that is unmindful,
Of righteousness careless, him I counsel
Again to turn him towards his thoughts,
His mind's fancy; then will he not fail
In his own bosom, buried deeply,
To find in his spirit righteousness sealed,
Amid the turmoil which ever troubles
His mind daily most and sorest,
And the heavy laziness that hampers his body,
And the heavy cares that quell a man
In mind and in spirit at every season.'

XXIII

Oh! truly blessed a man would be
Here in all things, had he the power to see
The bright and spotless heavenly stream,
That grand fountain of every good;
And if from himself he might hurl away
The dark mist, his spirit's darkness.
Yet now it behoves, God us helping,
With tales of fancy, fables ancient,
To amend your mind, that you more surely
May by straight course come to heaven,
To that spot eternal where our souls have rest.

XXIV

I have feather-wings fleeter than a bird's,
With which I may fly far from the earth
Over the high roof of the heaven above us;

But oh! that I might your mind furnish,
Your inmost wit, with these my wings,
Until you might on this world of mortals,
On all that there lives, look down easily!
Then you might mount on pinions
Straight over heaven, soaring upwards
Wind through the clouds, and then witness
All from above. You could also fly
Over the fire that long has fared,
Many a year, mid air and heaven,
Even as the Father at first appointed.
Then could you after the course follow
That the sun takes between the lights of heaven,
And onward speeding reach the sphere
Far up aloft; then in order
That star all cold, alone in station,
Which is the highest of heavenly bodies,
By sea-dwellers beneath the sky
Saturn called; cold is that star,
Wholly ice-bound, and highest wanders
Over all others up in heaven.
Yes, even then, when you have passed
High over Saturn, you may still journey,
And then will soon be above the sphere
That swiftly turns; and if straight you go,
Leaving behind you the highest heaven,
Then may you at last in the true Light
Have your portion, whence the sole Prince
Above the firmament far sway holds,
And also beneath, over every creature,
Guiding the world. A wise King He;
'Tis He that controls through all countries
All other kings over the world.
He with His bridle has firmly bound
The whole compass of heaven and earth;
With His guiding reins well He governs
And ever steers with mighty strength
The hastening car of earth and heaven.

He is the only Judge, in justice steadfast,
God unchanging, fair and glorious.
If you should reach by the right way
Up to that region, that right noble place,
Though for a time you have it forgotten,
Yet if again ever you thither arrive,
Then will you call out and quickly say:
'This, this only is mine own true home,
My land and country; from here am I come,
Here was created, by the Craftsman's might.
From here will I never take me away,
But pleasantly here it is my purpose,
The Father willing, firmly to stand.'
If to you after it shall ever befall
That you will, or may to this murky world
Come once more, you will quickly see
That all the unrighteous rulers of earth,
And all the mighty, those men so haughty
That most oppress this weary people,
Are ever themselves utterly wretched,
In all things feeble, failing in might,
Even these proud ones that this poor folk
Now for a season so sorely dreads.

XXV

Hear now a tale told of the proud ones,
The kings unrighteous that rule over the earth,
That shine among us with wondrous sheen
In many various beautiful vestures,
On high seats raised even to the roof,
Decked with gold, adorned with jewels,
On all sides hemmed with a countless host
Of thanes and fighters. These too are furnished
With battle harness of wondrous brightness,
With gleaming brands stoutly belted,
And with high state they serve the other,
Obedient all; and then, forth bursting
To every quarter, crush with force

All other nations that neighbouring dwell;
And their lord heeds, who the host rules,
Friend nor foeman, life nor fortune,
But ruthless ever rushes on all men
Unto a mad hound most has he likeness,
Too high uplifted within his heart,
For the dominion that each of his darlings,
His friends so trusty, aids to found.
If a man, however, might pluck from the tyrant
Each several garments of the royal garb,
And from him sever the various servants,
And likewise the power that once he possessed,
Then might you see that he is most like
To one of the men that now most busily
Press about him in painful service;
He might well be worse, but I think no better.
If such an one ever, all unwitting,
Happened to lose by lack of fortune
State and raiment and ready service,
And the power also which we have pictured:
If any of such things he sees no longer,
I know he will fancy that he has fallen
Deep in a dungeon, or himself he deems
In shackles fastened. This I may show,
That from over-measure in any matter,
In food or in dress, or in wine-drinking,
Or in sweetmeats, sorest waxes
The mighty frenzy of fierce desire
That clouds sore the inmost spirit
Of every mortal. Thence come most often
Evil pride of heart and profitless strife.
When rage is burning, within their bosoms
Their hearts are whelmed with waves enormous
Of seething passion, and soon thereafter
Are gripped in turn with grievous gloom,
Firmly caught. Anon there comes
Hope deceitful with hateful lying
Crying vengeance, for anger craves

More and more; then makes promise
The heart so reckless, of all right heedless.
I told you before in this same book
That somewhat of good by each single member
Of the wide creation is ever craved,
By the natural power that it possesses.
The unrighteous Kings that rule the earth
To no good ever can give an issue,
By reason of the sin whereof I have spoken
Nor is that a marvel, for they ever are minded
Themselves to abase, and bow to the power
Of each of the evils named already.
Needs then straitly they must submit
Unto the bondage of those masters,
The chieftains by them already chosen.
Yet is this worse, that a man will not
Resist this mastery even for a moment.
If he were ready to begin to wrestle
And the war thereafter to wage for ever,
Then were he never worthy of blame
Even if beaten, bested at last.

XXVI

I can from fables feigned of yore
Tell you a story touching nearly
This same matter whereof we speak.
In times long past once it betided
That prince Aulixes had possession
Under the Caesar of kingdoms twain.
He was the ruler of the realm of Thracia,
And Retia also ruled as chieftain;
And his liege lord's name, known to the nations
Was Agamemnon, ruler of all
The Greekish kingdom. It was common rumour
That in those times the Trojan war
Was fought under heaven. That hard fighter,
The Greekish monarch, marched to the field;
Aulixes likewise led five-score ships

Across the sea-stream, and there sat down
Full ten winters. Then the time came
When they had won the realm by war,
And the Greekish prince had dearly purchased
The town of Troy with his true comrades.
Then when to Aulixes leave was given,
The Thracian chieftain, thence to journey,
He left behind him of his horned barks
Nine and ninety; none of them thence,
Of these sea-horses, save only one,
He ferried over ocean, a foam-washed galley
With threefold oar-bank. Then came cold weather,
Raging storm-wind; the dun waves roaring
Dashed together, far out driving
Into the Wendelsea the warrior crew,
Upon the island where Apollo's daughter
Had been dwelling for many a day.
This same Apollo was of princely race,
Son of Jove. This Jove was a king
Who to great and little lying feigned,
To every goodman, that he was a god
Most high and holy. Thus this hero
The silly people pleased with error,
Till countless folk his feigning trusted
For he was rightly the realm's protector,
Of royal birth. 'Tis known abroad
That in those days each folk deemed
Its sovereign head the Highest God,
And gave him honour as King of Glory,
If to be ruler he was rightly born.
Jove's father also was further a god,
And the sea-dwellers Saturn named him,
The sons of men. Soon folk named
Each in turn God eternal.
Men say there was also Apollo's daughter,
Well descended, to witless mortals
A goddess seeming, skilled in magic,
In witchcraft dealing and in the delusions,

More than all men, of many a nation.
She was a king's daughter, Circe was called
Among the multitude, and she ruled men
Upon the island to which Aulixes
Chief of Thracia had chanced to come,
In his ship sailing. Soon was it known
To all the troop that tarried there with her,
The prince's coming. Then Circe herself
Loved beyond measure that lord of seamen,
And in the same way with all his soul
Such love for her he felt in his heart
That to his country no care to return
Had power in his mind like that of the maiden;
But he went on dwelling with the woman thereafter.
So long remained that none of his men,
His servants sturdy, would stay with him longer.
But after their hardships for home were longing,
And purposed to leave their dear lord behind.
Now folk began to make a fable,
How that this woman with her witchcraft
Changed men's bodies, and with baleful arts
Caused them to take, the king's true servants,
The bodies of beasts, and bound them afterwards,
And fastened many in fetters also.
Some became wolves and no word could utter.
But from time to time took to howling;
Some were wild boars, and broke into grunting
When they their sorrow sought to lament;
Those that were lions let forth in anger
A dreadful roar when they desired
To hail each other. These hapless mortals,
Both old and young, yes all, were turned
To some wild beast, such as before
During his life-days each most was like
All save the king, the queen's beloved.
Nought would they taste, any one of them,
Of meat of men, but more they longed for
What beasts supports, as was not seemly.

No more was left them of men's likeness,
Of the earth-dwellers, save only reason.
Each of them kept his own mind,
But this with sorrow was sorely beset
For the sad troubles that had assailed it.
Now the foolish ones that in this witchcraft
So long believed, in lying stories,
Notwithstanding knew that no one
The wit of man nor his mind can change
With magic art, though this be able
Mortal bodies for many a day
In form to worsen. Wonderful is it
And mighty, the power that every mind
Has over the slight and sluggish body!
You may by such examples see most clearly
That every cunning and craft of the body
Come from the mind in every man,
Each single power. It is easy to see
That to every man more harm brings
Wickedness of mind than weakness of body,
Of the frail flesh. Let none of the folk
Deem it possible that this poor flesh
May ever the mind of any mortal
Utterly change to its own estate.
Nay, 'tis the faults, each mind's failings,
And the inward purpose prompting each man,
That bend the body to their bidding.

XXVII

Why should you harass with wicked hatred
Your spirits weary, as the waves of ocean
Set a-tossing the ice-cold sea,
Urged by the blast? Why do you blame,
Your fate reproach that she has no power?
Why can you not bide the bitter coming
Of common death by God created
When he is drawing each day towards you?
Can you not perceive that he is ever pursuing

Each thing begotten, of earthly bearing,
Beasts and birds? Death also is busy
After mankind, all over this earth,
The dreadful huntsman, holding the chase;
Nor will he truly the trail abandon
Before that he catch at last the quarry
That he was pursuing. Oh! it is pitiful
That borough-dwellers cannot bide him,
But luckless mortals like the race of birds
Are flying onward fain to meet him,
Or as beasts of the forest that are ever fighting,
Each one seeking to slay the other.
But it is wicked for any creature
That towards another in his inmost temper
He should hatred bear, like bird or beast
But most right it were that every mortal
To others should render their due reward,
To all earth-dwellers, whatever they earn
By their life-works. He should love, that is,
All true men most tenderly,
And spare the wicked, as we have said.
The man himself he must love in mind,
And all his vices view with hatred,
And cut them away as best he can.

XXVIII

What man that learning on earth lacks
Does marvel not at the moving clouds,
The swift heavens, the stars' wheeling,
How never ceasing they spin around
The mass of earth? Which of mankind
No wonder shows at these shining bodies,
How that some of them a lesser space
Of course revolve, and others run
In longer circle? One of these lights
Is by world-men the Waggon Shafts called.
This a shorter course and journey keeps,
A smaller circle than other stars,

For it turns about the heavenly axle
At the northern end, nigh revolving.
On this same axle all is circling,
The spacious heavens are swiftly speeding,
Southward rushing, swift, untiring.
What earthly mortal does not marvel,
Save the wise ones who knew before,
That many stars a motion wider
Have in the heavens, some, however,
Run more straitly round the axle's end,
And move more widely when round its middle
They urge their race? One of these orbs
Is Saturn called; in some thirty winters
He girdles round this globe of earth.
Boötes also brightly shines,
Another star that to his station
In years as many moves round,
Even to the place from which he parted.
What mortal is there that marvels not
How that some stars sink in ocean,
Under the sea-waves, as men do suppose?
Some also deem that the sun does so;
But none the less false is this their fancy,
For neither at even nor in early morning
Is he nearer the ocean than at high noon.
Yet do men deem that he dives to ocean,
Into the sea, when he sinks to setting.
Who in the world wonders not
At the full moon, when in a moment
She is robbed of her beauty beneath the clouds,
With darkness covered? What mortal cannot
See with wonder the ways of all stars,
Why in bright weather they beam not forth
Before the sun, when such is their custom
In the middle of night before the moon,
When clear is heaven? How many a man,
At all such things sorely wonders,
But marvels not that men and beasts,

Every creature, keep up anger
Great and useless, each against other,
Never ceasing? It is a strange thing
That men do not marvel how often amid the clouds
The thunder sounds, then for a space
Lies silent; and likewise how
Waves and sea-shore are warring ever,
The wind and billows. Who wonders at this,
Or at another thing also, why ice is able
To come from water? When the sun shines
Hot in splendour, soon it hastens,
The wondrous ice-pool, once more to its kind,
Even to water. No wonder seems
To any of mortals what he may see
Day by day; but the crazy people
What they see but seldom sooner marvel,
Though to the minds of men of wisdom
It seem much less matter of wonder.
To unsteadfast men it ever seems
No part of the ancient early creation,
What they see seldom; but still they think,
World-men hold that by chance it happens,
Newly befalls, if to any before
It has not appeared a pity 'tis so!
But if any of them ever becomes
So lusting for knowledge that he begins to learn
Wise ways many, and the Warden of Life
From his mind clears the mountain of folly
That has buried it and abode with it long
Then I know well that lie will not marvel
At many a thing that now to mankind
A sign and a wonder everywhere seems.

XXIX

If you desire deeply to learn
The lofty power of the world's Lord
With clear understanding, consider diligently
The stars of heaven, how they ever stand

In lasting peace; long have they done so,
Even as the Prince of Glory has prepared them
At their first forming, so that the fiery one,
The sun, may not approach the cold one's path,
The moon's marches. Lo! the mighty orbs
Cross not the one the course of the other
Until it has fleeted far on its way.
Nor will that star ever seek in its journey
The west of the heavens, to which wise men give
The name of Ursa. All other stars
After the sun sink with the heavens
Below earth's base; alone he bides.
It is no wonder; he is wondrously near
The higher axle-end of the heavenly sphere.
Then brightly beams one star beyond others
That soars in the east, the sun preceding;
Him the sons of men star of the morning
Call under heaven; he heralds day
To men in the boroughs; then he brings
The glorious sun, the same day for all.
Fair and shining is the forerunner,
East up-leaping the sun he leads;
And again after the sun to his setting glides,
West under world. When night comes,
His name the nations change for another,
And then they style him Star of evening.
More swift than the sun, once they have set,
He speeds past him, that star all noble,
Until over again in the east he rises,
To men appearing, the sun preceding.
Those noble orbs night from day
By the Lord's power have fairly parted,
Sun and moon, in high peace moving
As from the first the Father appointed.
You need not fear that these fair ones
Will ever be sated with this their service
Before doomsday come. Therein He deals,
Mankind's Maker, as Him meet seems;

For he suffers them not, the Sovran God,
To be at the same time on one side of heaven,
Lest they ruin the rest of creation.
But God Eternal all things guides,
The broad creation, in bonds of peace.
Dryness sometimes drives out wet;
Whiles they mingle, by the Master's craft,
Cold and heat. To highest heaven
The flame all bright sometimes flies
Light through the air, behind it leaving
The weight of the earthly, though for a while
The cold earth closely within herself kept it
Held and hidden by the might of the Holy,
By the King's commandment. Each plant comes,
Brought forth by earth every year,
And the heat of summer for the sons of men.
Every year yields and drys
Over land's wide surface seed and leaflet.
Harvest offers to hands of mortals
Store of ripeness then rain and hailstorm
And snow too comes, soaking the ground
In time of winter, when fierce is weather.
For earth receives every seed-grain,
And makes it swell every season,
And in the spring-time leaves are sprouting.
But the kind Master for mankind's children,
To all that grows gives nurture,
To fruits in the world; brings them forth
When He chooses, Chief of heaven,
And them discovers to the dwellers on earth,
And anon removes, mankind's Saviour.
The Highest Good on His high-seat
Sole King sits, and this world spacious
Does His service; all His subjects
Thence He rules with His reins of leading.
No marvel is this He is God of multitudes,
King and Lord of all that lives,
Fount and First Cause of all His creatures,

Maker and Worker of this our world,
Law and Wisdom for the livers therein.
All His creatures upon His errands
From here He sends and hither bids.
Had He not established each so steady,
All His creatures, every one of them,
Breaking away had burst asunder,
In deadly hate had come to naught;
Yes, like foes they had fallen apart,
Though one love only all things created
In heaven and earth have in common,
That such a Leader they serve together,
All of them glad that the Father rules.
No need for wonder, for no one thing
Could ever hope to hold its life
Unless all were serving their common Source,
With all their might, their glorious Master.

XXX

In the East Omerus among the Greeks
Was in that country in songs most cunning,
Of Firgilius also friend and teacher,
Of that famed maker, best of masters.
Now this Omerus often and often
On the sun's splendour spent high praises,
His noble powers showed to the people
In glee and story, again and again.
Yet the sun cannot beam, for all his brightness,
Over all creation nor anywhere near it;
And even those creatures on which he can shine
He cannot illumine with equal light
Inside and out. But the Almighty
Ruler and Worker of the world's creatures
His own work overlooks;
All creatures alike He looks over.
He is the true Sun, and rightly so;
Such in His honour we may sing truly.

XXXI

You may know, if you will notice,
That many creatures of various kinds
Fare over earth with unlike motions,
With gait and colour quite diverse,
And aspects also of endless kinds,
Queer and common. Some creep and crawl
With all their body bound to the ground;
No wings them help on feet they walk not,
Nor pace the earth, as was them appointed.
Some on two feet fare over the ground,
Some are four-footed; some in flight
Wing beneath the clouds, Yet each creature
Is drooping earthward, stooping downward,
On the ground looking, longing for earth,
Some need-driven, some through greed.
Man only goes of all God's creatures
With gait upright, gazing upwards.
This is a token that he shall turn
His trust and his mind more up than down,
To the heavens above, lest he bend his thoughts
Like beasts earthward. It is not meet
That the mind of a mortal should remain below
While his face he holds up to heaven.